THIS BOOK BELONGS TO:

_____

DATE:

_____

graceful

The Graceful Leaf™
MY SEASONAL JOURNAL
Winter

SHERILYN S. LONG

THE GRACEFUL LEAF, LLC
www.TheGracefulLeaf.com

Cover and interior design by Sherilyn S. Long

Fonts and images provided by Canva.com

ISBN 979-8-9914455-1-1

The information in this book is not intended to diagnose, prescribe, prevent, or treat any condition. This is not meant to be used in place of qualified medical advice. Consult your physician before adding any supplement to your diet.

To the turkey gang at Tubb's Hill. Even during the bitter cold you reminded me of the importance of gratitude, confidence, and community. The first time I saw a wild tom turkey crash into a tree, I was amazed by your strength.
And I think you are happy to be admired!

...And to Tim, my hibernating bear. You are my favorite.
Thanks for being my warmth during the cold.

"The snow fell softly,
like a hush,
making the world
feel as if it were
holding its breath."

–KATE DOUGLAS WIGGIN,
REBECCA OF SUNNYBROOK FARM, 1903

Winter

the
graceful
leaf™

Introduction

"Let Autumn Go." I was half asleep and awake when these words drifted in like a gentle breeze. In the seasons of my life, I have learned an important lesson: "When the Spirit speaks, you listen." Any time you pour over creating, there's a bit of yourself placed into your creation. Each word and each line have heart, soul, and prayer etched into its pages. The Graceful Leaf™: My Seasonal Journal has been that for me. But like the colorful autumn leaves—masterpieces of color that must drop to move on to that next season—so, too, has it been my undoing, my aching, hesitating, and learning to let go. Winter has its many gifts, but to receive them, we must learn to let go.

Thomas Wentworth Higginson once said, "How many lessons of faith and beauty we should lose if there were no winter in our year!" It is for winter that our lives are richer and filled with meaning. Without its powerful lessons, creativity, and restfulness, we suffer. Winter is a kind, but powerful and necessary teacher.

Autumn leaves mulch and compost the trees. Masterpieces are laid down to decompose, but in doing so, they nourish the roots, providing a safe place for critters to nest and rest during the coming cold. Winter can be considered an inconvenience. In busy and frantic cultures, slowing down does not come easy. I admit I'm not much for slowing down either, but my cells call out for it. With a shift in understanding, winter becomes a thick, cozy blanket you can curl up under and find deep, satisfying rest. But you have to heed its call! Whether you like it or not, winter reminds us to stop fighting with reality. Winter teaches humility.

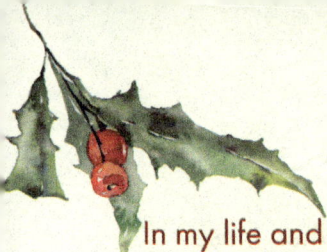

In my life and with my clients, I have seen the ill effects of nonstop producing and pleasing. A friend gave me some words of wisdom: "Life speaks in a whisper, a kick, a brick, and then a brick wall." Winter is the buffer between the whisper and the brick in the face. It's an opportunity to learn those lessons, to plan and shift as needed, to reflect and restore. Rest is a necessary part of a healthy life. I learned this in graduate school when I did not stop and ended up burned out with chronic fatigue, chronic inflammation, and autoimmunity. If we do not learn to stop and listen, not only do we get sick, but we can suffer in all areas of our lives. We owe it to ourselves and to the people in our lives to learn how to pace ourselves and say "no." Winter is the ultimate lesson on healthy boundaries.

Growth is desirable. But growing is not the only measure of success. How you grow matters! Winter is about strengthening. Trees that grow too fast are weak. Slow-growing trees have more winters to create strong rings. Buildings made with wood from slow-growing trees will last far longer than their quicker-growing counterparts. Seasons of healing take time. Just like seasons of growth and rest, the quick fix is not always the best. In pacing ourselves, we learn resilience. Winter makes us stronger.

No winter is the same, but there are general themes and lessons, whether your winter is snowy, wet, or maybe just a little more mild than usual. In my youth, I lived along the equator in the Philippines. We did not have the cold and snow, but for the astute observer, we did have seasons. As winter approached, the humidity dropped, and the weather cooled just enough to be bearable for visitors traveling abroad. At this time, we celebrated with lights and gatherings, just like the winter celebrations in many parts of the world. It was only after moving to North Idaho that I understood the celebrations of light as darkness faded. Days here are filled with cold and darkness. Winter teaches us to treasure warmth and light.

In the days of winter, bands of turkeys have wandered our streets. As animals huddle together, people also find ways to gather. Cold is relieved when we huddle together by firelight. Winter teaches us the importance of community.

Having moved to a snowy land, one of my first observations was that things don't happen on your own time. Perhaps they never did. We know autumn comes and goes, then winter follows. But the precise time when this happens is uncertain. We may see signs of these changes, but nature does not keep to a set schedule. You can't rush nature. At any other time of the year, we may live under the illusion of control, but when winter shows up, it's as if the whole community understands that best intentions mean nothing when wind and weather are at play. Driving up to a four-way stop and pumping my breaks, I slowly slid through the intersection, past a police officer. I threw up my hands, and we both smiled at each other. It was then I learned to love winter. Perfectionism gone. Winter teaches us grace.

Waiting is a necessary part of life. Winter teaches us powerful lessons of patience and faith. We have a better understanding of life when we patiently allow ourselves to pause, rejuvenate, and repair. Balancing the outer and the inner life, winter teaches us that not everything valued can be seen. It is the breaking down of the leaves, the soil microbes at work in winter

that feeds the soil and makes life possible. Winter teaches us the importance of the under-the-surface life.

The Graceful Leaf™, once colorful and showy, in winter, is broken down in the soil. But there are still invisible threads at work. In the air, under the surface, and in the seed down below. Did you know that in one square foot of soil there are potentially 1,000 seeds waiting for the right conditions to bloom? For many of those seeds, a cold, wet winter is a necessary step for moving forward.

This winter is unlike any other winter you may experience. As you cultivate the soil of your heart and utilize the pages of this winter edition of *The Graceful Leaf™: My Seasonal Journal*, I hope that, just like those 1,000 seeds waiting, you discover the value in this season, and from here, the vast possibilities from season-to-season as you live the graceful life!

How to Use this Journal

While it is helpful to learn from books about each season,
I believe there is no better way to learn this rhythm than to
experience and reflect on those changes. This is why I created
this seasonal journal. Winter is a perfect time to listen, watch,
reflect, and connect. Life is full of marvelous metaphors that
have the power to change and transform. It is my hope that
you return to these journals, discovering each year and each
season new levels of insight and growth. I have designed these
journals as an interactive experience. It is titled My Seasonal
Journal for a reason—I want you to fully immerse yourself in the
seasons and utilize this in YOUR transformation during this piv-
otal time. You will never experience this day, this winter, again.
What you do with it has the power to produce seeds that will
grow in the future. And this time of rest is vital for the growth.

In our world, we tend to look at the flashy new thing, but that
can be distracting. Sometimes, the best remedy is the most
simple one. It is not the far and remote or novel and new that
provides that healing transformation. What if the thing you are
looking for is so simple that it's obvious to a child—the crunch-
ing leaves, the picking of a flower, the amazement of watching
a squirrel store up its food for the winter, breathing in fresh air,
and digging in the soil?

So, pick up your journal and a pen, take a moment to walk
outside and ponder. You are a walking miracle and are
held and loved so deeply. You are at home in our world.

Can you SEE it?
Can you TASTE it?
Can you HEAR it?
Can you FEEL it?
Can you SMELL it?
Can you SENSE it?

Then let's begin!

graceful

The Sit Spot

One of the best ways to connect with the seasons is to establish a sit spot in a natural setting. You will visit this place every day, ideally at the same time each day. The goal is to allow yourself to slow down your body and mind and observe. Watch and listen! Even when you are in the city, nature is all around you. Find a place to cozy up, watch and listen, and be part of nature.

This winter, if you live in a cold climate, you may choose to take a familiar walk instead, or if you grab a blanket and something insulated to sit on, you may choose to brave the cold. Feel the crisp air and notice temperature and light changes. Even if you live in a warmer region, you may notice the weather is just a little cooler than at other times of the year. The goal is to get in tune with your region and, more specifically, with one mini-ecosystem. Pay attention to the temperature changes, light and dark, insects and animals, and watch the plants and their gradual changes. Allow yourself to awaken your senses!

Planning Ahead

Today's Date: _____

What are you looking forward to this season?

Do you have any plans or projects in the works?

Do you have any trips planned this time of year?

Who do you want to connect with during this time?

What emotions or feelings do you want to have this season?

What do you want to bring in this winter?

What do you want to let go of?

Winter Memories

What is your favorite winter memory? What smell brings this favorite memory to mind?

What is your favorite winter color? Why?

What Is your favorite winter sound? why?

What is your favorite meal or drink to cherish during this season?

Do you have a winter tree, plant, or animal story?

Do you have a meaningful winter weather story? What were the lessons you learned from that experience?

Do you have a favorite winter memory that reminds you to slow down?

graceful

FIRST DAY OF WINTER:
December 21st

WINTER'S FOCUS:
Soil, Strengthening, and Rest

WINTER'S MESSAGE:
Life is a marathon and not a sprint.
For resilience, you must have rest, repair,
and rejuvenation.

WINTER'S CRITTERS:
Animals have shed their summer coat, gained weight, and gained their thicker winter coats to keep warm. Those that don't migrate alter their diet. Deer, elk, and moose thrive on twigs and branches and heartier foods. If they eat more nutritious food left out by good-intending humans during the winter, it hurts their stomachs and digestion and may end up causing their demise. Diet is specific to region and temperature and changes with the seasons. Herd animals such as deer, elk, and moose migrate down the mountains and closer to civilization. Some animals, like grey squirrels, have stored their food for the winter and prepared ahead. They have built warm nests, only venturing out for food when the weather is milder. Birds have migrated to the south for warmer weather during the winter, while other true hibernators like bears, chipmunks, woodchucks, and ground squirrels remain curled and inactive in their dens, relying on their bodies' fat stores to get them through the majority of the season.

"When it snows,
she has no fear
for her household;
since all of them
are doubly
clothed."
–QUEEN BATHSHEBA AS TOLD
TO HER SON,
KING SOLOMON, PROVERBS 31:21, CJB

The Graceful Leaf™ Journal

Winter leaves

The Graceful Leaf™ Journal

Winter kiss

Winter leaves

Winter leaves

Winter leaves

Winter leaves

The Graceful Leaf™ Journal

Winter leaves

Lessons From Winter

- Enjoy your harvest. Celebration is important!
- Wisdom invites us to prepare ahead for dark and cold days.
- If you feel your energy wane and need rest, give yourself grace.
- Plan your garden. Consider and percolate on what you want to plant again.
- Cultivate creativity and color.
- Celebrate and share your bounty with others.
- Marvel at the dark and celebrate the light. Enjoy the stars and cultivate awe.
- Nurture community and family.
- Enjoy quiet and stillness.
- Focus on warming yourself and others.
- Retain and maintain heat, expel coldness and dampness.
- Hydrate and moisturize. Find and foster boundaries and protection.
- Eat mild and warming foods; focus on building up health.
- Read, journal, and reflect. Now is your time to curl up with a good book.
- Enjoy soups, starches, meats, fats, and stored foods.
- Monitor your sugar consumption, and switch out your sugars for healthier alternatives to keep your immune system up.
- Focus on strengthening and slowing down.
- Celebrate the soil, dig into motivations and dreams.
- Focus on supporting the kidneys and the bladder, digestion, and elimination.
- Most nutritious plant parts are underground—find your nourishment by diving deep.
- Gaze into the fire, feel its warmth and reflect.

- Feel the full spectrum of emotions and release trapped emotions.
- Just as enjoying bitter herbs will warm you, when you learn to integrate from hard experiences, you will be warmed by what they can create.
- Nourish yourself with warming herbal teas.
- Give others grace and understanding.
- Focus on communication, forgiveness, and reconciliation.
- Let go of toxic emotions, routines, and tasks that drain your energy.
- Set boundaries. Our busy culture counters the rest of creation at this time.
- Avoid overindulging. Your biology is thinking scarcity during winter and will hold onto weight.
- Maximize your sleep.
- Gentle exercise and indoor movement.
- Supplement with vitamin D3.
- Bundle up and get outside. Fresh air and sunlight are good for you!
- Eat more fermented foods. Fermenting foods increases vitamin C content.
- How you process and preserve your learnings will increase your nourishment.
- How you clothe yourself matters—invest in clothing that keeps you warm and dry.
- What seems like loss or decay is only a necessary transition.
- Nothing is ever wasted or lost.
- Celebrate variety and color.
- Slow down and savor.

REMEMBER: DURING DARK DAYS, THE LIGHT WILL BREAK THROUGH AGAIN. THE COLD IS NOT FOREVER. BIG THINGS ARE HAPPENING UNDER THE SURFACE, EVEN NOW.

"New beautiful things come in the first spit of snow on the northwest wind, and the old things go, not one lasts."

–CARL SANDBURG,
"Autumn Movement," 1918

The Graceful Leaf™ Journal

Winter drifts

Winter leaves

Winter leaves

Winter leaves

Winter leaves

Winter leaves

Winter leaves

The Graceful Leaf™ Journal

graceful

Now Is The Time For...

ENJOYING
Your Harvest

PLANTING
A Winter Garden
Turnips
Carrots
Beets
Cabbage
Kale
Spinach
Radishes

GROWING
Indoor Herbs
Parsley
Chives
Rosemary

SAVING, SORTING, AND STORING
Seeds

PLANNING
Your Next Garden

STARTING
Indoor Seeds

PRUNING
Fruit Trees

HARDENING
Plants Before Planting Outdoors

"There is no sign of
leaf or bud,
A hush is over
everything -
Silent as women
wait for love,
The world is waiting
for the spring."

–SARA TEASDALE,
"CENTRAL PARK AT DUSK," 1911

Winter leaves

Winter leaves

The Graceful Leaf™ Journal

Winter leaves

Winter leaves

The Graceful Leaf™
Journal

Winter drifts

Winter leaves

The Graceful Leaf™ Journal

Winter kiss

Winter leaves

Herbal Love

PINE
(PINUS SPP.)
LEARNING STRENGTH, RESILIENCE, HUMILITY, FAITH

Pines are evergreen, coniferous trees with needlelike leaves, displaying their green, tufted needles and demonstrating continuity throughout the seasons and in every region. Pine trees are resilient and adaptable in various terrains, elevations, and climates, thriving in every continent except Antarctica. There are 187 species of pine, 49 species existing within North America. Pines range from 3 to 80 meters (10 to 260 feet) tall, living between 100 and 1,000 years. Pine branches, needles, and cones grow in a spiral pattern, following the Fibonacci sequence known as "the golden ratio" or "nature's secret code." Pine needles are in tufted bundles, typically between 2 and 5 needles (except for the Singleleaf Pinyon Pine, which only has one needle per tuft).

Pinecones consist of pine pollen cones (male) and pine seed cones (female). Pine pollen cones are small, contain the new year's growth, and release large amounts of pollen in the spring. Pine seed cones are more prominent and thicker and drop once they release their seeds. Some pines also contain "fire cones," which stay tightly contained and encapsulate wax that would release in the event of fire, serving as the tree's protection in such an event. Then, they release seeds to reseed after a forest fire.

Pines tend to thrive in sunlight and are less abundant in shady conditions. They are often the first tree species to increase after a forest fire and specialize in regenerating low-mineral soils. Some pines, like the Ponderosa Pine, have mechanisms to survive fire conditions, such as large needles that drop their lower branches as they mature. Some pines tend to thrive in difficult situations.

All parts of every pine tree are edible and medicinal—the young, soft pollen cones and pollen, white inner bark, cambium, seeds, roots, resin, and young needles. They can be added to soups, sautéed, steamed, or boiled. Pine is an excellent source of vitamin C, treatment for respiratory infections, kidney support, and a great source of protein and B vitamins. Pine pollen, collected in the spring, is a superfood used to increase energy and longevity, balance hormones, promote tissue regeneration and skin health, prevent wrinkles, and increase libido. Pine resin is loaded with B vitamins and is an excellent antiseptic. Pine bark improves circulation and blood vessel strength. Pine nuts are a traditional food source and make an excellent milk alternative. Pine needles, collected year-round, are high in vitamins C and A. This amazing gift of a tree is worth being thankful for!

Pines teach the value of humility. Native American tribes used pine needle infusions to survive harsh winters, treat fevers and coughs, and prevent scurvy, and they shared their knowledge with humble settlers who had asked for assistance. However, proud settlers that did not seek help and wisdom died under the same pine trees that would have saved them.

And, of course, Pine trees provide homes, raw materials, and food for critters both large and small during the long winter months.

NOTE: Make sure you identify your plants correctly and seek out local plant guides for identification and proper usage before utilizing any wild edible or medicinal plant. The yew tree (which is not a pine and contains flat needles and red berries) is the only lookalike and is toxic to humans and animals.

"Nature looks dead in winter because her life is gathered into her heart. She withers the plant down to the root that she may grow it up again fairer and stronger. She calls her family together within her inmost home to prepare them for being scattered abroad upon the face of the earth."

–HUGH MACMILLAN,
"THE MINISTRY OF NATURE," 1871

Winter drifts

Winter leaves

The Graceful Leaf™ Journal

Winter leaves

Winter leaves

Winter leaves

Winter leaves

Winter leaves

Herbal Tales

The pine with their long, tufted needles are master weavers, threading together the continuity of life and the seasons. I grew up climbing trees in the Philippines, but my first memory of pine trees was when I was in sixth grade in the U.S., a time when my mother was being treated for breast cancer. We returned to be close to family, to rest, and recover. While there, we went as a family to visit and stay at a beautiful farm called The Apple Orchard. As kids, we played, picked fruit, and meandered around the property. I swung on tree branches and discovered delectable grapes hidden under a web of layered green hands. I hugged trees and drank in their terpenes, wild and free. It was there that I discovered the wonder of pine.

Mesmerized, I discovered the smallest pine cones and also a massive 1.5-foot-long sugar pine cone (grows up to 2 feet in length). I was inspired! I collected my prizes and brought them back home with me, relics from a healing pilgrimage. Arriving triumphant at home, I showed them off to the much younger second-grade neighbors and declared myself the founder and leader of The Pine Cone Club! My rulership was as tall as the pines, my ego the size of its massive cones. It lasted only two weeks before the little minions created an insurrection and started their own club, leaving me humbled with my precious collection.

No matter what was going on in my world, when pines were nearby, I always felt peace. During this time, to escape during mom's cancer treatments, I crawled under the pine tree displayed in our winter home, smelling its sap and staring up the tree at the layered lights and decorations.

Mom survived her treatments, but in my high school days, she fell ill again and passed away. During those days, it was the pine trees outside our home that sustained me, gave me their perfumed strength, tall sentries of loving continuity during change, loss, and sadness.

I have shared pines with my own grandkids and in my practice. We explore the wonder of a pinecone, wrapping our arms around and burying our noses in the vanilla-scented bark of the Ponderosa Pine. We experience the thrill of these master weavers, continuity in the midst of change. I now share these wonders on herb walks and to anyone who will listen. Winter reminds us to let go. But pine reminds us that nothing is ever lost.

STRENGTH, RESILIENCE, HUMILITY, FAITH

"Time will change it,
I'm well aware,
As winter changes
the trees."

–EMILY BRONTE,
WUTHERING HEIGHTS, 1847

The Graceful Leaf™ Journal

Winter leaves

Winter leaves

Winter leaves

The Graceful Leaf™ Journal

Winter leaves

The Graceful Leaf™ Journal

Winter leaves

The Graceful Leaf™ Journal

Winter kiss

Winter leaves

graceful

Winter Medicine

MAKE AN INFUSION
FLOWERS, LEAVES, BERRIES, SEEDS, BUDS
AND SENSITIVE PLANT PARTS AND CONSTITUENTS

Infusion. (N.) Origin. Late Middle English. From Latin. infūsiōn-, infūsiō-

A liquid extract prepared by soaking herbs or tea leaves in water. Infusions are made using the delicate parts of a plant or when you want to utilize heat-sensitive constituents of a plant, such as vitamin C. While pine needles have less delicate plant parts, they are high in vitamin C, which is sensitive to heat and starts to dissipate once a plant has been picked. Other evergreens or plant parts like rosehips and orange peel, known for their vitamin C content, are best when using the infusion method (stronger plant parts are best prepared using the decoction method).

PROCEDURE

Add one tablespoon of fresh cut herbs or one heaping teaspoon of dry herbs to a mug. Boil one cup of water, then pour over the herbs, cover, and steep for 10 minutes or more. If you increase the amount of herb or extend the steeping time, you will increase the strength of the herbs. Some herbs, like pine needles, require a larger amount of herb (1/4 cup) per cup of water because they are much milder.

Winter Friendly Herbs to Use

American Mountain Ash, Aspen and Cottonwood Buds, Astragalus, Bayberry, Birch, Brigham Tea, Burdock Root, Citrus, Cranberry, Dandelion Root, Dulse and Edible Seaweeds, Fir, Ginseng, Ginger, Jerusalem Artichoke, Juniper, Maple, Marshmallow Root, Pine, Rosehips, Sassafras, Spruce, Squashberry, Staghorn Sumac, Willow, Wintergreen, and Yarrow.

"*Nature is full of genius, full of divinity; so that not a snowflake escapes its fashioning hand.*"

–HENRY DAVID THOREAU,
"JOURNAL ENTRY," JANUARY 5, 1856

The Graceful Leaf™
Journal

Winter drifts

Winter leaves

Winter leaves

Winter leaves

Winter leaves

Winter leaves

Winter leaves

The Graceful Leaf™
WINTER KITCHEN

PINE AND PEPPERMINT WINTER CHAI RECIPE

2 cups water
25 cloves
3 cinnamon sticks
1 T. cardamom pods
2 1/2 T. fresh ginger (or 1 1/2 T. ground ginger)
4 black peppercorns
1 T. astragalus root, cut and dried
1 T. ashwaganda root, cut and dried
1-2 Tbsp. orange zest (or 1 Tbsp. dried orange peel)
1 T. peppermint, cut and dried
1/4 cup fresh cut pine (or fir) needles
5 cups coconut milk or your preferred milk (I have used rice milk
and almond milk)
1/2 cup honey

Using a Saucepan: Place water and all spices (except peppermint, orange zest, and pine needles) in a saucepan and simmer for 10-20 minutes. Reduce heat and add peppermint, milk, and honey. Heat until it simmers. Turn off the heat before boiling point, cover, and steep for 10 minutes. Strain and serve.

Using a Crockpot: Heat on low for 1-2 hours until steam forms. Reduce heat to warm and add the other ingredients. Continue to heat on warm for 30 minutes or until steam forms again. Turn off the heat and steep covered for 10 minutes. Strain and return to the cleaned crockpot. Enjoy!

Serves 5-6.

FOR THE LOVE OF CHAI

Chai is a traditional Indian favorite. It is typically made with black tea and sugar. Chai is a wonderful warming drink for wintertime, soothing and warming the body and assisting digestion. Cardamom, cinnamon, cloves, ginger, and peppercorns are common chai ingredients. They are all excellent digestive supports, warming and helping strengthen the immune system. This caffeine-free herbal alternative utilizes soothing peppermint, ashwagandha, and astragalus. Peppermint is an antispasmodic, anti-inflammatory, and digestive support that soothes stomach aches and calms the nerves. Ashwagandha is known as an adaptogenic herb that helps to balance the body and alleviate chronic stress. Astragalus root is a strengthening and immune-boosting herb, excellent during winter.

While you may focus on living seasonally, which helps to mitigate stress, cultural stressors occur during this season. With the feasting and tendency to overeat during these winter gatherings, drinking this chai is an excellent way to support yourself and your family's digestion and immune system and help to relieve stress; perfect for winter. I made a variation of this chai for my husband while we were dating, and I credit this recipe for "making" him fall in love with me. Combine it with standing under the mistletoe; you may be surprised by the magic and feelings of love that ensue!

This recipe will utilize both a decoction method for hardier herbs and an infusion method for gentler herbs, thus preserving the vitamin C content of the orange zest and pine needles.

NOTE: Omit astragalus during an active cold or coughs. While immune boosting during times of health, during times of sickness, it can worsen the condition.

"If we had no winter, the spring would not be so pleasant: If we did not sometimes taste adversity, prosperity would not be so welcome."

-ANNE BRADSTREET,
MEDITATIONS DIVINE AND MORAL, 1655

The Graceful Leaf™ Journal

Winter drifts

Winter leaves

The Graceful Leaf™ Journal

Winter leaves

Winter leaves

Winter leaves

The Graceful Leaf™ Journal

Winter leaves

Winter leaves

The Graceful Leaf™ Journal

Winter Reflections

Reflecting on this season...

WHAT HAVE I LET GO OF AND
LAID TO REST?

Winter Reflections

Winter Drifts

Reflecting on this season...

HOW HAVE I EXPERIENCED
WARMTH THIS SEASON?

Winter Reflections

"Let us love winter, for it is the spring of genius."
— PIETRO ARETINO,
THE WORKS OF ARETINO, 1926

Winter Drifts

Reflecting on this season...
WHAT PLANNED OR SURPRISING PROVISIONS HAVE I EXPERIENCED?

Winter Reflections

"In seed time learn,
in harvest teach,
in winter enjoy."
— WILLIAM BLAKE,
THE MARRIAGE OF HEAVEN AND HELL, *1793*

Winter Drifts

Reflecting on this season...

WHAT AM I LOOKING FORWARD TO CULTIVATING MOVING FORWARD?

Winter Reflections

"The trumpet of a prophecy!
O Wind, If Winter comes,
can Spring be far behind?"
— PERCY BLYTHE SHELLEY,
"ODE TO THE WEST WIND," 1820

Winter Drifts

Sometimes we just have to get rid of the lines!

WAYS I HAVE FOUND GRACE THIS SEASON:

DRAW A PICTURE OR SHARE AN IMAGE TO HIGHLIGHT THIS SEASON:

by graceful leaf™

graceful

Reflect on the Changes...
WHAT TRANSFORMATION HAVE
YOU EXPERIENCED THAT IS WORTH
CELEBRATING? WHAT SIGHTS,
SOUNDS, AND FEELINGS
HIGHLIGHT THIS SHIFT?

"See! The winter is past; the rains are over and gone. Flowers appear on the earth; the season of singing has come, the cooing of doves is heard in our land."

— KING SOLOMON
SONG OF SOLOMON 2:11–12 NIV

Did you get to...

play?

If you enjoyed this journal
I would be so, SO grateful if
WRITE A REVIEW...

THE
GRACEFUL LEAF™

SO WHAT EXACTLY IS THE GRACEFUL LEAF ™?

Defying gravity, The Graceful Leaf™ hangs, suspended by an invisible thread, halfway between heaven and earth. Purely medicinal, this gift of nature feeds the body and soul and is a constant reminder that no matter what happens in life, you are always held by a love that has given you <u>everything</u> you need, right here and now, to

LIVE THE GRACEFUL LIFE!
2 Peter 1:3

ABOUT THE CREATOR

SHERILYN S. LONG, MH, C.Ht. is an author, speaker, and life coach located in beautiful North Idaho. She is also a Master Herbalist who is passionate about connecting others with the natural world and supporting them in their healing journey.

Sherilyn's love for nature was always evident, from her days of growing up in the Philippines and time spent climbing trees as a child, to her pursuit and discovery that using natural methods would heal her from chronic fatigue, brain fog, and neurotoxicity that impacted the use of her right hand. Sherilyn now helps others find hope and healing, reminding people that God made them for a garden.

TheGracefulLeaf.com

If you enjoyed this journal
I would be so, SO grateful if you'd
WRITE A REVIEW...

It's easy and gets this journal into the hands of more people.

STEP 1: Go to AMAZON.com
STEP 2: Search for my book in Amazon books.
STEP 3: Scroll down to REVIEWS
STEP 4: Leave a Review

I'd love to know your thoughts and hear what
you got from your journal!
Contact me at: sherilyn@thegracefulleaf.com
www.facebook.com/sherilynslongauthor
www.instagram.com/sherilynslongauthor

Join my newsletter for more info on
events and releases.
Sign up here: www.TheGracefulLeaf.com

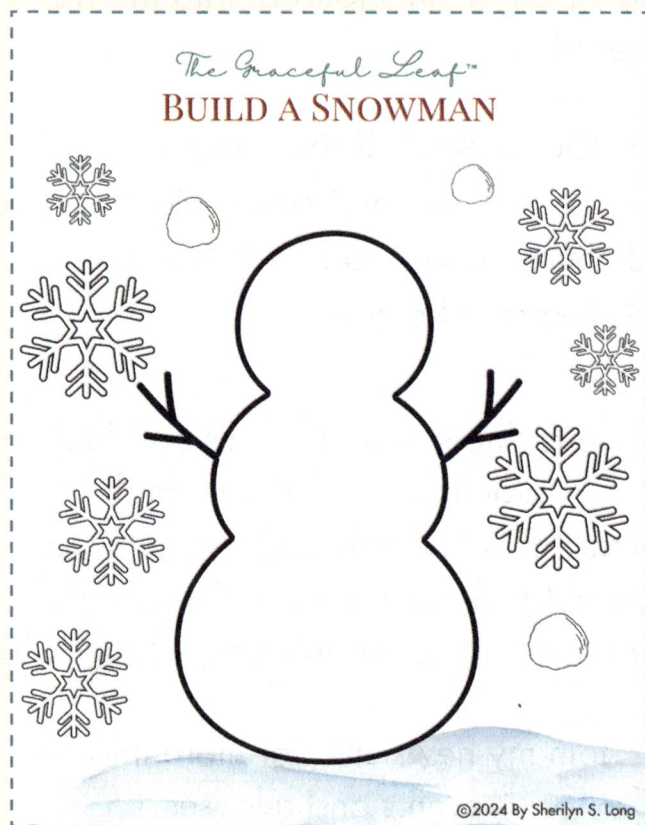

The Graceful Leaf™
BUILD A SNOWMAN

©2024 By Sherilyn S. Long

**ACTIVITY
AND
COLORING PAGES**

ENJOY YOUR NEXT
SEASON WITH...

The Graceful Leaf™
MY SEASONAL JOURNAL

Spring

HOW WILL YOU LIVE THE GRACEFUL
LIFE THIS COMING SEASON?

More From the Author

Sherilyn S. Long

THE GRACEFUL LEAF™ MY SEASONAL JOURNAL

The Graceful Leaf™
MY SEASONAL JOURNAL

Autumn

SHERILYN S. LONG

The Graceful Leaf™ MY SEASONAL JOURNAL

Spring

SHERILYN S. LONG

Find these books at www.AMAZON.com
or TheGracefulLeaf.com

THE
GRACEFUL LEAF™

Made in the USA
Monee, IL
12 January 2026